Illuminative Rhymes

Lilian J Walters

Presentation by *BookLeaf Publishing*

Web: www.bookleafpub.com

E-mail: info@bookleafpub.com

ISBN: 9789358738452

First edition 2023

*For mom, dad, Carol and Olivia, my
reasons for being here.*

ACKNOWLEDGEMENT

For everyone I've ever met and communicated with in this life, especially the people who helped me find my flame, you have contributed to the formation of this work and for that I am eternally grateful...thank you.

Additional gratitude goes to the AC/PI, who have greatly influenced my quest for the divine spark. If any of you read this, I hope it is as worthy of your time as your work was to me.

PREFACE

First of all, allow me to thank you for acquiring this work. I hope it brings you joy and inspiration, as well as hopefully offering you a different perspective on themes for poetry and writing.

For the longest time I have deliberated, hesitated and procrastinated. I have always been interested in writing and said that one day I would get something published, but never knew what. If my life was a school report it would say "has lots of potential but lacks consistency". I have flown through life by the seat of my pants so far, and it was only when I found the challenge from Book Leaf Publishing that I realised there was something I could give back to the world. It might not be a bestseller or top of anyone's must-read list, but it's a piece of work that I'm proud of, a way of leaving my mark.

For me personally, I have always struggled with the notion of purpose and "the bigger picture". Everyone I know seems to have it all figured out, but I have been late to the party on many occasions. At this period in my life, I'm starting to see that writing may be what I am here for. The Egyptian god Thoth gave us the gift of the written word, the Greek god Hermes was also a silver-tongued messenger from the heavens. I would like to think, in some small way, that I have been able to pay homage to those deities with this work.

You may read this and be able to relate it. You may read this and enjoy the rhyme schemes. You may read it and wish you'd bought something else instead (although I'd sincerely hope not!) Either way, I am thankful that I have an ability I am able to share with the world and I really do hope you enjoy it.

Opening Limerick

A man tried to think of a poem
Of what, there was no way of knowing
The man scratched his head
This came out instead
So it looks like he'd better get going.

The Attention Seeker

Listen up, admire me,
Here I am, here,
You can't see the irony,
Confidence dressed in fear.
Disguised as a person,
Collected and calm,
My condition has worsened,
See the sweat on my palm,
I just want you to see me
Here in all my true glory
Take a look at me, really,
You're gonna love my story
Once upon a time
An idea was born
An imperfect crime
At the breaking of dawn
His rays would shine down
And the world was bright
There was never a frown
When the sun was in sight
But he soon had to set
And the people would mourn
The moon paid his debt
As she blew her own horn
Alas, but a few heard the sound

As everyone else would sleep
It went off once but it was all around
Primordial, booming and deep
Realising her call was a failure,
The moon faded into the mist
She was as beautiful as a dahlia
That bloomed when the sunlight kissed
The solar song was vibrant
And the world danced to its tune
The cruel demands of a tyrant
Compared to the humble moon
Until one day the sun would shine
And the moon would block it out
"They're not just yours, they're mine!"
The moon began to shout
The sun was rendered powerless
As the world started to see
By the timing of an hourglass
The moon had authority
The people stood in awe
Of the lunar goddess's might
Two hours passed, three, then four,
Still the sun was barely in sight
Eventually the moon relinquished
And the great golden light returned
But now the world recognised and distinguished
That even the darkness burned
So the moral of this tale
Is that light can cause you to miss

The inner strength you should hail
That can be found in the abyss.

Depressive Questions

Dark clouds start to form over a blue sky
I feel so empty, but I can't figure out why
My life is good, everything should be great
Could it be all of the sugar I ate?
Is it the fact that I don't drive a car?
Or my career plans haven't gotten that far?
Could it be that I'm an only child?
Was my innocence early on completely defiled?
Did my parents not love me enough?
Did they do their best even though life was
tough?
Why do I distance myself from my friends?
Would they forgive me if I tried to make
amends?
I choose to sit alone in this room
Turn my back on the sunshine and welcome the
gloom
Is depression a choice or a long-term affliction
Like disease or some kind of terrible addiction?
Can I snap myself out of it and just be happy?
Am I a 40 year old still wearing a nappy?
Did I run from the challenges I was meant to
face?
Life is a marathon I didn't expect to race

Am I battered and bruised from remembering
every scar?
Does anyone ever know how resilient they are?
Does my face show you the magnitude of my
pain
From reliving the events that have scrambled my
brain?
Do I muster my smile with knowledge or
blindness?
The best way to kill your enemies is with
kindness
But what do you do with the harbingers within?
The ones that reside just under your skin?
The first step is admitting that there is a fault
The Eureka moment strikes like a lightning bolt
My smile becomes real as I begin to cry
Because I'm depressed, and now I finally know
why.

While...

While injustice and chaos reigns
While we're led by the least among us
While exist corporate chains
While they infect us like a fungus
While these idiots pull our strings
While the puppet masters pull theirs
While we're bothered by status and things
While they have no such cares
While prices keep on rising
While the news is Depression Tourette's
While everything is downsizing
While everyone's hedging their bets
While money becomes obsolete
While the planet is sponsored by coffee
While the plan becomes complete
While hungry mouths get frothy
While disease is big business
While entertainment is bigger
While innocents ask "what IS this?"
While the guilty pull the trigger
While people bury their heads
While their souls get fleeced
While spiritually we're dead
While we're banned from the feast
While some wait till the end

While some choose to go quicker
While some try to pretend
While some are even thicker
While the rich ARE laughing at you
While you think you're laughing with them.
While jailers don't have to catch you
While you've created your own prison.

Revalue all values.

The Addict

One more time
One more rhyme
Feels so good
Just like it should
Hit my spot
What have you got?
That's it, there
I just don't care
Stay, don't leave
I don't wanna grieve
No wait, please
I'll beg on my knees
Dammit, you're gone
I just wanted one
One more throw
One more go
I feel so cold
This habit is old
I just need to quit
That's the hard bit
I'll give it a try
Just before I die
No, do it now
That's just it, how?
Just use your mind

Let it unwind
Let yourself breathe
Let your thoughts weave
A web of resilience
Show me your brilliance
Ok, I'll do it
That's it! I knew it
See? You are tough
And you are good enough
Don't let it win
Don't give in
I'm doing just fine....
...

...

...

Ok then, one last time.

Limerick Interlude

You might find this stuff a bit weird
Like a goatee without a beard
But give it a go
Because you don't know
If you'll rethink the themes you once cheered.

Nonsense Rhyming (or How to get Order from Chaos)

Chicken in a basket
What would you ask it?
Crumbs on a table
As it tells you its fable
Purple pillars hold up the place
Like a robber with a mask on his face
Where's the love?
It comes from above
So below
Where angels fear to go
Rhyming is easy
Sometimes it's cheesy
It takes years of stuttering
To articulate the spluttering
Playtime is done
There's no more fun
Joy is fleeting
When your head's taking a beating
Cleanup on aisle 6
Where everything clicks
Like a specialist pen
Made by specialist men
The ink flows freely
Have I finished yet? Nearly

Put it on the page
The sorrow, the rage
The nonsense, the mess
The worst, the best
Turn word salad origami
Into eloquent salami!

Knowledge

Where did you get all your knowledge?
How do you know so much?
Did you have to dig and forage
Or did you hear it from such and such?
They say that knowledge is power
I say it's a gift and a curse
It can make a sweet man sour
Or send a woman from bad to worse
They say that you need to practice
Continually to get better
People mock and say "you won't hack this"
And opinions like that can fetter
Knowledge isn't always useful
But it depends on what you know
It can make your mouth run like a loose stool
Or it can help your plants to grow
Every day is a school day
The class is always in session
You can teach yourself in a cool way
Or completely ignore the lesson
It isn't just experience
That informs your education
The news provides expedience
The media, revelation
Thesis, antithesis and synthesis

As once cited by Hegel
Is how you really get "into this"
And take it to the next level
Lather, rinse and repeat
As the dialectic demands
To grow is no mean feat
To marry up all the strands
Of a complicated existence
To bring it all together
Requires great persistence
And skin as thick as leather
You will appear small to those
Who have no wings to fly
You'll cut off your face to spite your nose
And nobody will wonder why
While on their laurels the victors are resting
The entire world is burning
And the mighty are subject to testing
Because they are always learning
To paraphrase a Jung man
"No consciousness without pain"
It will lick you like a tongue can
And then grind you down again
Nobody said life was facile
Newsflash: it's goddamn tough
But it's completely worth the hassle
When you realise you don't know enough.

The Root of All Equals

In the beginning, all men were created equal
Yet some people think they're the prequel and
the sequel
Your money doesn't really make you a happy
bunny
And your name's not synonymous with the
game, player
You'll get more toasts when you're close to the
ghosts
A jacket made from phantom fabrics
While all we get is flat bricks thrown at us to
dodge
You eat bourgeois caviar, we gobble up stodge
Unless you're stackin' dough nobody wants to
know
How much did you spend, how much did you
blow
It doesn't matter because one day you'll die
And you'll never have looked that person in the
eye
Did you see his struggle, did you witness her
plight?
You wanted for nothing, for everything he had to
fight
An easy life isn't life because life isn't easy

So jeez, please don't try to appease me
You see, money is nothing in this game of
existence
I'd say it's all about overcoming resistance
Britain's Got Talent, and it's milked for a profit
Worthwhile financial causes? Come off it
We're all human, just some of us are more
human than others
Some of us would even step over our own
mothers
It's the root of all evil and everyone's infected
Thank God it's only the poor who are protected
Your eye results are back.... You have £20/£20
vision
Time for you to make a decision
Casharact surgery or the blind leading the blind?
It doesn't matter anyway, nobody will mind
Sit and count your chips like they're your best
friend
The reaper will come for us all in the end.

The Paradox

I rub the lamp and the genie appears
Grants me 3 wishes but I only have one
He offers me riches, power and status
Instead I ask for that which cannot be done
I wish for a paradox I can solve in 5 minutes
The like of which is too good to be true
The genie cocks his head to the side
Then he disappears and I'm sat here with you
A familiar stranger from a memory never had
We talk, we touch, we kiss, we love
Not knowing whether things are good or bad
It feels like an eternity has passed
But the timer on my watch says 4:59
And I shudder as the paradox is revealed
Our utopia becomes asinine
The happiness is replaced with an impossible
demand
The stranger inevitably turns to dust
A black hole pulls the essence from my soul
Extracting my core, leaving only a husk
I crash to the floor a lifeless heap
Broken, alone, all hope is gone
But the stranger remains by my side
And I know the love inside lives on
My heart fills with light once again

I overcome every pain and cramp
I stand up and behold a wondrous sight
I take a deep breath and reach for the lamp...

Haiku Interlude

Trees rise up through soil
Standing proud in the forest
Bright beacons of hope.

Smaerd

My head's in the charcoal-coloured clouds of
heaven
I don't seem to mind
The sun lies like a fiery Armageddon
Its heat as welcome as death
I'm trapped in complete freedom
A voluntary patient in the Dream Asylum
A world that's real when you see them
And nightmares are written, directed and starred
in
This Stockholm syndrome is true
I really don't want to leave
So sick in the head that I spill my guts too
So much so that the pain feels like rapture
This place of haves and have-nots makes me
question,
"Who makes the rules here?"
Oh yeah, I do, that's my reflection
Tied to a stock, stripped bare with no safe word
Who's enjoying this more, me or you?
I feel primal, carnal, urgent
A brain with a beast that can reason too
Take this all away from me
And I'll fill the void faithfully
I'm not even protesting any more

Just take the wheel and pray to me
After all, it's only part of the show
I've worked so hard to achieve this pain
Don't cheapen it with illusions and tricks
One day I'll tie the game
Until then, I'm getting lost in your image
I will gaze on your all-perfection
Close my eyes and wander
Doing justice to my selection
As I lull myself back to sleep.

Less

When voices become voiceless
People become choiceless
Frogs in the throat that were placed by reptiles
Scaly, slimy, slithering things
That sit astride the food chain

When hope becomes hopeless
People become worthless
Dreams that were dashed by suits and ties
Profiting from losses that lost profits and
prophets
Placing the blame at their doors

When teeth become toothless
People are powerless
Stripped of dignity and replaced by conformity
Given uniforms by self-titled officers
Who take with one hand and shy the other

When children become childless
People become purposeless
Slapped in the face by a grim reality that tests
the purest of hearts
Following the wide path to evil
Detracting from the heroic tunnel

When society becomes fearless
The rich will become helpless
Shaking off the self-imposed shackles of
resignation
True meritocracy involves all and not one
Ensuring a bright future for one and all.

Reality Show

Look at me, I'm on TV
Let me show you what I can do
I can sing, dance, beg on one knee
All the while entertaining you

My background is humble but in all of my
dreams
I knew that one day I'd become a star
My home life came apart at the seams
But I'm more prepared for fame than you are

Lots of new friends, parties, new lifestyle
Seems like I've come a long way
It's all codswallop, trash and bile
That's what my old mother would say

Look at me, I'm a role model now
The whole thing feels like a great big joke
Pondering, struggling to understand how
While I drink, take lots of drugs and smoke

I wanted all of this for so damn long
But now I find myself disappearing
Why is this dream all going wrong?
Why are none of my fans cheering?

No more am I in the papers
Nobody even wants a picture
I've been in prison for some of my capers
But the jail of my mind is a permanent fixture

Look at me, I'm on TV
I'm gone but hopefully not forgotten
Overdosed and dead at 23
Their dreams made my reality rotten.

Criminal

My words are like stainless steel knives, they'll
stab you
My message is like open hands, it'll grab you
This verbal assault is an urban assault
Breaking in and raiding the vault
It's a crime that I wrote this thing behind bars
But these words will take your soul to Mars
It's a long stretch before my expirement
But all I'll miss is my own retirement
I'm trapped in this cage like a beast in heat
There's nothing I can do to make ends meet
This life ain't easy, I've learned that and more
I'd say that I've earned myself an encore
Even though I didn't get any applause
I'll know I'm the best as I leave through the
doors
People walk around like their unlocked screens
No substance, just a bunch of posts and memes
No panache, no class, no style, no fire
When will we see some flames of desire?
It's 2023 and the world's beyond repair
Money is in charge and no-one seems to care
It's definitely the endgame, we've had the snap
The planet gone because we didn't have its back

When will we stand up and take back what's
ours?
A world where the virtuous have the powers
We just need to talk to each other, nothing more
No need to make it a political war
There exists a Third World, but for what?
An entire population treated like snot
Education costs thousands but distraction is free
That really doesn't sit well with me
Let's fix this planet and start from scratch
We could make this life better for all with no
catch
Equal opportunities for every child
No more privilege running wild
The Earth governed by the just and fair
It's gonna take time but I know we'll get there
The voice of the nation has got a sore throat
Time we realised we're all in this boat
Unite all people in every region
As one we are defeated, together we are legion.

Limerick Interlude 2

Let's try and keep things light
It's only poetry, right?
Pick it up, put it down
Have a smile, have a frown
Just let your mind take flight!

A Day In The Life of the Overman

Stretched over the abyss
Is the rope of man
I walked across
Like no other can
I own myself
I am slave to none
I have no interests
Save for one
I am the best
Because I know my mind
Unlocked all the contents
I could find
At first I was shocked
Slightly appalled
Then I got brave
And became enthralled
To know ourselves
We must know who we're not
To revalue all values
The things that we've got
We keep what's useful
Get rid of the rest
Small price to pay
To try and be the best

To overcome yourself
Is no easy task
To find your identity
When to put on the mask
To know what you like
And give it your all
To pick yourself up
After countless falls
To put your selfish feelings aside
Or own them
And walk through Hell with pride
You see, we're all angels and devils
The lines get blurry
On various levels
To choose one path
Is to ignore the other
Embrace the void
And call him brother
Travel both roads
And you will go far
Find out exactly
Who and what you are.

Temet Nosce - Know Thyself.

Haiku Interlude 2

Skies filled with sunshine
Waves crash into wholesome rocks
The near perfect storm.

Limerick Interlude 3

A soul once reincarnated
On a planet it thought that it hated
It learned all it could
And reached the godhood
Because now its appetite was sated.

Superheroes Are Liars

Show me a nurse who works a 12 hour day
Who has young kids and still finds time to play
Who goes to uni to make their lives better
To escape the stigmas and be a go-getter
Show me a man who follows his dream
To play for a professional football team
But gave it all up when things hit the skids
Because he prioritised love for his wife and kids
Show me a drifter who had no drive
A guy whose life seemed to be in a dive
Until his girl gave birth to his son
Now his family blooms because they're second
to none
A self-made man who's climbed to the top
Who came from the bottom and vowed not to
stop
He loves and fights with all his heart
Who makes living life look like an art
Show me a woman who struggles with words
But finds immense beauty in flowers and birds
She gives it her all for her man and her daughter
The human equivalent of bricks and mortar
You see, these people are real heroes
Keep your Schwarzeneggers and Robert De
Niros

Bye bye Batman, keep walking Clark Kent
Too much time on hero worship is spent
These people deserve to be hailed by the masses
To hear the clinking of champagne glasses
Well here it is, to you, I raise a toast
Because you are the people who inspire me the
most.

Closing Haiku

Hearts filled with wonder
The beating of a snare drum
Love's eternal song.